Sânziana Batiște

THE STAR SIGN OF THE WOLVES

Poems

Translated into English by Diana-Viorela Burlacu

eLiteratura

Front cover image: Dakota, a grey wolf at the UK Wolf Conservation Trust, howling on top of a snowy hill. Image Credit: Retron | http://en.wikipedia.org/wiki/File:Howlsnow .jpg
Cover design: Leo Orman

eLiteratura

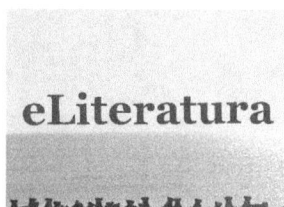

www.eLiteratura.net
www.eLiteratura.com.ro
ISBN-13: 978-606-700-236-2 (eLiteratura)

[This book can also be acquired in Kindle format, via Amazon.com.
The Kindle format ISBN:
                    978-606-700-237-9.]

For more information about this book
please write to info@eLiteratura.com.ro *or*
info@ePublishers.info.

THE STAR SIGN OF THE WOLVES

Poems by Sânziana Batişte

Translated into English
by Diana-Viorela Burlacu

Sânziana Batişte

Who is the Author of This Book?

SÂNZIANA BATIȘTE (pen name of Maria-Felicia Moșneang, born in Brad, Hunedoara) is a poet and writer. Member of the Writers' Union of Romania.

Volumes:

The Star Sign of the Wolves, 1999;

Lambs of Light, 1999;

Doinas and doras, 2001 (Clusium Publishing House, Cluj-Napoca);

Sweet Arizona, 2002 (Călăuza Publishing House, Deva);

Meadows of the Deities. Haiku. Les pâturages de dieux, 2007;

Beneath-the-Sky Room, 2007;

The Star Sign of the Wolves. Farkasok csillagjegye, translated by/ forditó: Simone Györfi, 2011;

The Star Sign of the Wolves, translated into English by: Diana-Viorela Burlacu, 2013 (Casa Cărții de Știință Publishing House, Cluj-Napoca).

Present in anthologies and literary dictionaries.

Information on life and work: the monograph *Candour and exile in Sânziana Batişte's poetry and prose*, by Ladislau Daradici, 2012, Casa Cărții de Știință Publishing House, Cluj-Napoca.

Who is the Translator of This Book?

DIANA-VIORELA BURLACU (née Ionescu, in Brad, Hunedoara), Ph.D., is a teaching assistant within the Department of Romanian Language, Culture and Civilisation at the Faculty of Letters, Babeş-Bolyai University Cluj-Napoca. M.A. in British Cultural Studies (2002), Ph.D. in Linguistic Studies (2010). Erasmus-scholarship holder at Southern University Odense, Denmark (1999-2000), BBU-scholarship holder at

Eberhard Karls Universität Tübingen, Germany (2009).

Volumes: *A Pragmatic Approach to Pinteresque Drama*, 2011, Casa Cărţii de Ştiinţă Publishing House, Cluj-Napoca.

Antonyms, Synonyms, Analogies. Minimal Vocabulary of Romanian Language – with an English Translation (coauthors: Gabriela Biriş and Elisabeta Şoşa), 2011, Saeculum I.O. Publishing House, Bucharest.

Antonyms, Synonyms, Analogies. Minimal Vocabulary of Romanian Language – with an English Translation (coauthors: Gabriela Biriş and Elisabeta Şoşa), second edition, 2013, Casa Cărţii de Ştiinţă Publishing House, Cluj-Napoca.

Author and coauthor of studies of pragmatics, lexicology and semantics.

Translations: *Ideea de sport în sculptură. The Idea of Sports in Sculp-*

ture, Dorin Almăşan (coauthor: Adina-Laura Fodor), 2007, Grinta Publishing House, Cluj-Napoca;

Zodia Lupilor. The Star Sign of the Wolves, 2013 (Casa Cărţii de Ştiinţă Publishing House, Cluj-Napoca).

MOTTO:

My right hand closes into the
                              book
and I'm entire here
my smile is entire –

From my death nothing will
                              ever
part me

(Sânziana Batişte – *Smile)*

TABLE OF CONTENTS

Borderland

Blank page – my secret
borderland
sole sea you welcome me
(oh, even drop by drop,
you welcome me)
to you I come

Misty shadows shroud me
again
their touch cold

and the things of the world
                    shiver
and set down with one more
                        lining

My translucent arms out
          towards the skyline
holding my soul on palms, up
slowly walking
with blind eyes
to the hidden murmur
serene
      even
            duskless

How He Was Calling Me

How that man was calling me
throwing my name up in the
                              sky
singing
or hissing it to me
as if to the serpents

How that man was waiting for
                              me

standing still in the moving
        lights of the destiny –
voracious fountain
and tender labyrinth

How that man was caressing
                    me
swimming in my eyes
coming adrift through my
              hair locks
and moulding me with the
              certainty
of the seer

How that man was
         resurrecting me

how he was losing me
here – now

Like never before

I Was a Tree

I was a thoughtful tree
                              praying
I was the blossom of the tree
                              as well
and the fruit

Unwedded scent
and the people

So in the silence of the world
                              beginning
I was asking for you

King

The Laughter of the Winner

Look – with a clumsy hand
I draw again words on my life

Yet may your regard come –
to your reading we shall be
                    obedient

Yet may your snowy hand
                    come too
and the bitter mouth

and the crying
and the breath flowing
           through the air

And the laughter
of the winner over the flags

Time

The fire crackles – freezing
                                silently

The copper of my bracelet
glides and uncoils snakelike
across the paper

Look at it now isolated in its
                                corner
waiting for its share of milk –

Poetry

So Much Pride

So much pride falling loose –
multicoloured balloons
ribbons
and drums
and trumpets

O-lé!

Where should I hide with my
humbleness
where – a pepper grain of
sadness

The shell of silence is broken

I roll through stones
into the uncaring ear

of the universe

They Like the Beast

They like the beast running
the slave falling
broken limbs, viscera
the eruption of blood
the shriek

What about the beast's neck
        on the caressing
        beast's neck?
What about the beast licking
        its offspring?

What about the beast at my
            feet sleepy-ing
(fluid sun in our twin blood
flowing)
the beast dreaming?

They like the beast

They Pass Conceitedly

They pass conceitedly in the
light –

Some admire
their babble with sibylline
pretensions –
the ersatz philosophy
the word orgies
the nerve explosion
the raving

the palaver in the mirror

Others see the king's clothes
acclaim frantically
and

The – retinue – slowly –
                          passes
(children with mouths
                     fastened, fingers
cut,
closed in the dark sigh)

They – pass – conceitedly –
                  in – the – light

At the Gates of the Word

At the Gates of the Word
at the throne of the Lord
I have also come on bended
                         knee
led from behind by the deity

I have washed myself from
                head to toes
with juice of word-sloes

Instead of garments
words
words

I have adorned myself
                    hecticly
full of joy, childishly

To dare I got drunk
with alms-words, a chunk,

I am now bowing and smiling
before the Throne of the King
cut and panting, my tongue
                    insane

(From the screaming cry I
                    abstain)

Since I Was Bound

Since I was bound
to stop resisting

Now may it come
light from light
effluvia –

words
words
words

I have started to be
your unquenchable lover

There Is a Time

There is a time
when pain fades away
content and amiable
like the triumphant lion

The universe breathes rarely,
                                    at pace,
(the beast rests)
and nothing hurts me

Only the grass of nostalgia
        burns inside the soul
like alcohol

I Am Not the Dust

I am not the dust of the
                    Wanderer
I would like to say –

But trembles with cold
                    shivers
the thought insane

I am not the dust of the
                    Wanderer
nor am I going to be –

But among star signs a ripple
                    passes –
too late it has to be

I am not the dust of whoever
                    lies to me –
I am crying in vain –
Somebody is laughing casting
                    before me

the one die

What a Beast

What a beast
what a foolish figure –
both woman and man –
The two-body-dweller heart
                              lit
the soul in one

In the sky of the scents lifting
twinned foreheads, two
but between them flickering
entire fields of dew –

The eyes warmly born to
                    wonders
never see each other
They sometimes open only in
                    dreaming
in a strange light
And they look at each other
incessantly they look at each
                    other
fantastic mysterious lakes
their waters bound deep, in
                    the depths
from the beginning of time

What a beast
what a foolish figure –
neither a woman nor a man –

How it laughs, how it cries
how it shivers
trembling

Abyss

Your soul I'd been searching
                    in words
the warm abyss
genuine perfume

Dwell, oh dwell
and may forever hurt me
the quick instant
the divine gift

Oh, descend me to this
eternity

Your soul I'd been searching
in words

It Is Night

It is night
in the sky and on the earth –
                    silence
spreading poisonous, slow
effluence

I am thinking of you –

How I keep silent
I could keep silent so deep
that I would also become
                    silence

the flowing silence

My eyes know how to be
                              silent
my hands
my mouth

If only my heart were not
beating
calling like a raving bell

unique reality
suspending me
on the frozen eye

of eternity

First Comes

First comes the tear
and washes me

Then comes the shriek
and blesses me

But afterwards the nightmare
                              comes
there comes the nightmare

how it humiliates me
God

How it humiliates me

Christ

Oh, Lord
these adornments
you put on me
how heavy

You yourselves
if I came
once again
would not recognise me
        under them

Your senseless
dreams
made me an icon
sheathed with precious stones

Who knows
who still knows
to listen to my heart
empty

Au clair de la lune

Au clair de la lune silence is
                 growing
in the sleeping houses peace
                 is falling
in the dimming eyes
                 sheltering light
in the hearts stepping to the
                 line of sight

Bizarre shadows light
                 mysterious fires

soul mates swim in them,
                 waters of desire

Boughs breaking?
Serene is the night

Clocks wailing?
Humble is the mind

Au clair de la lune who
                 passes away?
Mon ami Pierrot
cold is my mouth, made of
                      clay

My Soul

My soul like a beast
alone in the desert like a
                              beast
my soul like a beast
swelling its nostril

How Patient

How patient the Desert
like a liquid spider flowing
confident like a Conqueror

How it wove its detestable
                    geometry
and imprisoned me to this
                    angle
of darkness

I stagger when it moves
                    heavily

sometimes I even struggle
exhausted

How patient the Desert
and how it despises me

after it doomed me

The Tree King

Tree with shaken boughs
long sap, long quivers
Flowers blooming afar
their scent reaching me
through the clouds ajar

The tree king – roots full of
                              blood
onto a shiny setting
(secret wars, lost armada
a conqueror smiling)

Tree in the middle of the
                    world ablaze
lover on earth
and in the skies' maze
and in the sacred waters

I
To you
who am I to you?

The Eyes

As I lie awake dreaming
the gates around closing

Darling
brother of mine – I groan
I feel cold
    I feel cold
        I feel cold
Do not make me the prey of
              her eyes

Rejoice, sister of mine

Who may She be – I want to
                    know
She has no name – you echo

And it's late
the eyes searching for me for
                ever and ever
the moon growing paler and
                    paler

My darling are you here? I
                sigh
a dead smile I smile
as I am being eyed

By the Unnamed She with
empty eyes

Dance

Dance
dance on tile
dance in the dark
dance on the void

A square
a triangle
my balance mark

Upper my soul
upper
Where nor human, nor beast

If only we learned
if only we learned
not to feel the grief

Dance
dance real
dance deluded
dance on glowing coal

Dance on life – dance on
                           death
dance on the altar

A Tear

A
tear
a naiad
lunatic body
   burning
   violent

But – the stone eye
and the stone mouth
and the stone nostril
and the stone brow

But – the stone eye
and the stone mouth
and the stone nostril
and the stone brow

What a world
artistic nightmare

Up to the Skies

Up to the skies and beyond
it should have been thought
it should have been uttered

Some wind with tears
bends my face to the east
to the west

Why does the god with snakes
          and flowers
turn to me and smiles

I am not I any longer
no one subject to its sad
                    errors

Bee from the flower
wax from the bee
light from the wax –
and so I ebbed away

He who does not believe it
shall search for me in vain
                    through

the infinity

Yet You Were the Beast

Yet you were the Beast
while I was the doubt

T'was raining Sodom and
                    Gomorrah's
over our offspring, ours

A Corridor

A corridor through the
                              rippling air
where I fall asleep
where you wake up
(oh, the moments flowing as
                              insane
in the riverbed of the same
                              tale)

Our murmuring proximity
(Here I and There you living)

And the breath – sniffing
                         hungrily

A tender halo around us
                    misting

Oh, I Was Saying

Oh, I was saying
in vain are you weeping
Nobody lighting from your
                          blaze
nobody burning
nobody crying
nobody for you longing

Nobody
Nobody

Your dream in stole
within it purl by purl

Smash it
Destroy it

I Was Wandering

I was wandering through
        lands of darkness
and I was weeping
Oh, alas to myself – I said
Oh, alas to myself

Then
suddenly
this unhoped-for wonder –

Countless
delicate windows open to
the temple of grass

And the green
the silky guard of lovers

lighting me

Oh, You Will Die

Oh, you will die, too – I say to
                              myself
showing in turns crooked
                              faces
broken mirrors
waving white shrouds

And then?
And then? my childish hopes
long for the Sequel

surrounding me with smiling
eyes
murmuring impatiently

lunatic hopes
barefooted hopes

wandering among stones and
flowers

The Suite of Colours

The suite of colours slowly
moves on the dial
and flavoured fruits humiliate
me again
speaking of secrets
which have peacefully passed
away

You blissful – I whisper
on the edge of the abyss

You blissful – I whisper
blinding
fading
and melting me away
in the air you are burning

Godly

The New Babylon

The new Babylon
over the old Babylon
  (There we sat down
  and wept)

A sea of fog
over a sea of smoke
  (The wafer in tears
  we cracked)

Words giving birth bright
gold-like
on the unlit – lit embers

And your solemn face
known – unknown
rising from them
lunatic

I Am Alone

I am alone in the lap of
                        eternity

Gently
hesitant
tormenting
the spirit of the linden flowers
touches my hair locks
blows me apart

Oh, I could die
(I beg for mercy)

But there is no mercy and
radiant
I sing alone in the lap of
                        eternity

Too Late

Fog buoys in the night
                    coming late
thrilled flavours gliding
coming from the noise of the
                    luring world
but always withdrawing
with a smile

How much loneliness has the
                    moon ground in
my hair locks

may it be redemption?

Grizzle like the times
here I am bound
to this wakeful, watching
endlessness

Unrelenting Sibyllas time my
life
and slide me to the realm
with sadness rife

It is much too late to die

and much too early
to wish to rise victoriously
and lonely

Hidden Within Commandments

Hidden within your
                    commandments
from century to century you
                show yourself

Yet the mouth fills with the
                    sand
of the bitter loneliness

Yet the mouth also bursts
                    with crying

the salty horizon flickers
the thought flickers
pale

Now
Never
Now
Never

Nausea I Feel

Nausea I feel about one dying
                unknown and

alone

lamented
by the gleam of the stars
at dusk

Nausea I feel of his unknown
                   betrayal

cold
wicked

like the deathly heavy sweat
on a star

Nausea I feel and
disillusion above all thrills me

Nausea I feel

Is this why
I have not sun-set yet?

Never

Never in the dark
Never in the dark

Ripped I tear myself from the
        saws of the night
and at the foot of the day
I fall

Self-Portrait

Watch our outstretched arm
begging like a branch of a
                    trunk – torso
turned to a sun glimpsed
now and then

The vague swelling of buds
speaks of an ecstatic spring

Until then
gently

we enter the scenery of

Endlessness

My Life, the Tear

My life was trickling
the tear
on the cold
translucent window

I was contemplating it
     carefully, more
     carefully,
(Silence – don't scream, I
     warned the child
whose eyes I saw open

in awe
in a bigger and bigger awe –
and they turned into
        precipices of awe
and then into abysses of fear
while his mouth clenched
while he became dumb)

Wolf Fangs

Wolf fangs glistening
on snow
on the asphalt

The moon chip
mingled
with the sun in bed

Wandering spirit
hungry heart

Barbarous love dooms me

Surge

Sensual surge
star pollen

Tender breath gliding

And the mild terror
of supreme exigencies

into a white kiss
demonising

The Keys

Lighted bough euphorically
                          smiling
(or maybe a charmed flute
a flute vanished from the
                          empire of time)

A scream crumbling
caught in the stream-like
                          arteries
within the breath like a
                          stream of

peace flowing

I am kissing you (I am
          throwing the keys)

Body smiling
I am kissing you

1978

Where From

Where does my body know
                    you from?
It is a stranger – I shout to it

But it like a beast
turns around lazily
and swelling its nostril
rips me

Rips me

I Form Myself

I painfully form myself within
you –

It is breaking
melting

it is disunion

Surprise
rising and decline

Alienation
unalienation

And the world flows above me
indifferently
when roaring under its tragic
                    splendour
I raise, towards the sky, the
                    meek face

of a lily-beast

Star Sign

Look – I knew
There was the Star Sign of the
                          Wolves

The star sign of the Wolf
                          brothers

The Wolves of the words
chasing their prey away
rifting the snow
defeated by a sacred hunger

Poor you – I was saying
Poor you – I was crying
yet at night they would howl
                                wildly

And a moon-struck bell tolls
incessantly
calling me under the moon

in the pack of the mesmerised

(Luceafărul Magazine, 1989, May 13)

Set-on Words

Set-on words
lashing me
ripping me –

Wolf tongues
wolf fangs
wolf howl buried in a
              perishing body

For a new birth –
for a star smiling

relentlessly

Thus the Sacrifice

Thus
the sacrifice has decided

The victim is free to go
free to breathe
free to laugh or to cry
in the thin air replete with
                              gods –

The torturer itself cries
while building her alive

in the death that rives her
with sweet linden flowers

The victim grows shy
when (once again) is likened
                  to Christ

The torturer smiles kindly
        and encourages her
singing godly

if not yet dead

You Wealthy Man

You wealthy man
how well you know to satiate
                                    me

You wealthy man
how compassionately you
                                    watch me

In your mansion house you
                        have me seated
at the head of the table

to feel repugnance to my
                              greed
you are unable

But my beastlike hunger
                              revives
(in turns you subdue me
and kneel to me)
You have put a tiara on my
                              brows

Yet I keep bleeding
under the heavy wreath of
                              thorns

Panta Rhei

Panta rhei – says the Poet
(since only a Poet could be
the one who suddenly felt a
                    glide into
the waves of the fluidal
matter,
a flight)

Pantha rei – I gladly repeat
in the evening, when tired the
            mirror mists over

when the walls of the room
      crushing impassibly
shroud me in their
      indiscernible powder
and I feel leaving
flowing
to the river where a face
lights on
fades away

deceitfully

You Have Cast Me

You have cast me to the deceit
  of this barbarous
  winter
There are no more innocent
  snowflakes on the
  earth

Only my own room
a huge snowflake
takes me from time to time
to an ancient season

as in an ancient vow –

Delicate grass
edenic triumph
still haunts me softly

Turned to wonders
I tear myself from winter with
                    a sigh

The Grace

Like a hallucinated forest, of
                    monsters –
the Inexpressible

And suddenly
the Grace above them
feeding them with the milk of
                    speech

transfiguring them

Blind

Blind
running
running
running

Tearing waves of darkness
printing the sky
with the bleeding
stubs
of the soul

With Stars

With stars pinned on my
                    temple
embraced by a cold light
I was dancing losing my life
forgetting what was
                    happening
In front of the white crystal
where, like in a chrysalis
the queen
of the great pyramid
was resting

With stars pinned on her
                    temple
embraced by a cold light
losing her life
forgetting what was
                    happening

Birth

My grace is drinking
slowly and mildly
like bison, from the water

and the mud is giving birth to
       water lilies of light

Voracious is the divine
                scenery
that turned me away

and tearing my garments of
                              clay
dying me out of life

it gave birth to me

The Life of Life

The life of life –
the taste of your words

When Everything is Here and
Now

When Everything lies beside
me
goes through me

We were
the Song of Songs –
smoke

How Close

How close to harmony
                everything is
foam or fruit
But the thread of my fate
no power I find to unknot

The wheat grain within
                     reshapes
The image of The One Who I
                         Am

Send me the sign, Lord
voice now

my passing on Earth

We Do Not See
Each Other

We do not see each other
deep is the night
but like the dream's dolphins
this poem breathes

Your lips will sip its breath
slowly, slowly
and I will feel

and I will endlessly know
that I can start again

to die

Side by Side Shall We Stay

Side by side shall we stay in
      the night's growth
and in the golden honeycomb
      of the mouth
step by step the light will
      divinely sprout

We shall look at each other
we shall smile in wonder

And the tear will light
                    remotely
approaching us redeemingly
It seems to us that nothing
                    separates us at all
but a translucent and light
                    wall

Burning fragrances in the
                    serene night
we shall feel soft doors open
filling us with sweet and
                    bitter delight

as if poppy flowers blossom at
                    twilight

But Only

But only
the bodies
swing
painfully
in an ocean
of bodies

Implacable Fruit

Implacable fruit

It is autumn
and we feel deep, in our
                              slumber
its roundness
of a sun
its open eye

enormous

There is so much pity
how we float slowly

sipped

Soothing us
deepening us

driving us into words

Rich I Am

Rich I am

The dreams' flock
would never stop
Oh, Lord
how it would never stop

And gifted I am with
                    expectancy

Oh, Lord
Thee I thank for so much
                    mercy

Yet between us lies the still
                    pointer
which life into death
death into life
changes?

We Were

There was a procession of
                          bison
There was a procession of
                          butterflies
There was a procession of
                          clouds

Which I was watching
contemplating
encircling
scattering

In the cloak of rays
joyful

we were a procession of
                    flowers

You May Miss

You may miss a humble
                    flower
(Has anyone seen it?
Has anyone glimpsed it?
Is it not only a myth?)

It may be away now
Maybe
to you it has never travelled
                    before

Pray

To you yourselves pray
so that it spring
It itself may miss you

endlessly

Running Point

Jingling masks
hilarious attire

White owls
carnival-like

Yet everywhere
the limpid lucency –

seed of the running point
burning ultimately

What It Knows

What my blood knows
will freeze
and will give itself to the
                    ground

What the hungry beast – my
                    spirit
feels
deeply feels

shall pass, will always repass

breath by breath
into the sacred vapour of the

Word

N.

It split into syllables
and offered itself as food
to the world mouths starving

Heavier and heavier pulsating
like a star
the hunger it within conceals

Resigned emperor
over the decaying world

sluggishly its name dashes

Will We Ever Satiate

Will we ever satiate
this sidereal hunger
digging voids
caving voids

calling from the bowels of the
                              universe
from the cathedral of the lily
and from the tomb of the
                              seashell

from the sacred
vain mouth of my
lover?

This hunger
and this thirst
to which we restlessly cast
our smile
our hopes
our humble and glorious
victories

and we ourselves
into the supreme leap

of poetry

Smile

Reckless I was searching for
you in my sleep

You were far away – you were
close to me
(I was sliding into the giant
iris of the nights
migrating under eyelids)

Death is life – I have started
to understand

My right hand closes into the
book
and I'm entire here
my smile is entire

From my death nothing will
ever part me

Slowly Grows the Light

Slowly grows the light
slowly grows the legend
    A – cornered – star – has –
                                unveiled

Now the birth is
Now the annunciation is
The star – in – the skies – has
                            – moved

But again
hopelessly
like a phantom gliding on the
                              line
of the horizon

a sandy day
a sandy day
a sandy day

Yet – slowly – grows – the
                              light

Salt

Yet I descending ripped by
the moonlight
Yet I crawling in stubs of
wings

Yet I going blind
and going dumb
and desperate
rising

lured by tunes

with powder on eyelashes
with a petrified smile

Yet I was there
and you knew it
Yet I was the salt

on – the – table – of – your –
feasts

Title: How I Play with a Wolf Cub / That I Dearly Hug

Poem:
– Good day, dear wolf cub,
                    pray
Where should I take you,
                    which way?

– To another fortress
untouched walls
no mourning

no longing
throne undescending

times not remembered
peace unmarred

– My dear wolf cub, join me
there I shall take thee

to unmarred peace
times not remembered

throne undescending
yet climbing stairs of longing
untouched walls

TO – ANOTHER –
       FORTRESS

http://ro.wikipedia.org/wiki
/Sânziana_Batişte

www.ingramcontent.com/pod-product-compliance
Lightning Source LLC
LaVergne TN
LVHW051739080426
835511LV00018B/3148